BALEEN

Written by Josephine Croser
Illustrated by David Kennett

ETA
Cuisenaire

Baleen
ISBN 0-7406-1018-X
ETA 352011

Revised American edition published in 2004 by ETA/Cuisenaire®
under license from Era Publications. All rights reserved.

Text © Josephine Croser
Illustrations © David Kennett

ETA/Cuisenaire Product Development Manager: Mary Watanabe
Lead Editor: Betty Hey
Editorial Team: Kevin Anderson, Kim O'Brien, Nancy Sheldon,
  Elizabeth Sycamore
Educational Consultant: Geraldine Haggard, Ed.D.

ETA/Cuisenaire • Vernon Hills, IL 60061-1862
800-445-5985 • www.etacuisenaire.com

Printed in China.

06 07 08 09 10 11 12 13   10 9 8 7 6 5 4 3

BALEEN

Once upon a time there lived a mighty whale, Baleen, the wildest raider in the sea. Baleen preyed upon other animals for food. He was fierce beyond reason and greedy beyond need.

It was forbidden for whales to fight each other, but that did not deter Baleen. He attacked Bluntt, another massive whale. The battle would change Baleen's life forever.

This is the story of one whale's quest for power and glory — and another's gift of forgiveness. In the tradition of the folktale, it explains why some whales have no teeth.

After reading the story, learn about interesting whale facts and vocabulary in the Appendix.

nce upon a time there lived a mighty whale named Baleen. Baleen was the wildest raider in all the seas. With just one whack of his tail, he could whip the water into foam. When he snortcd, spray rose like steam right up to the clouds.

Baleen, like all whales of that time, wa[s] predator. But, Baleen was fierce and gree[dy,] taking more than he needed. Nothing pleas[ed] him more than to wrestle with his prey. Whe[n] the battle was over, he would sing a song o[f] pride, gloating that *he* was the strongest of all.

Baleen moved through the water like a huge black shadow, searching for things to conquer.

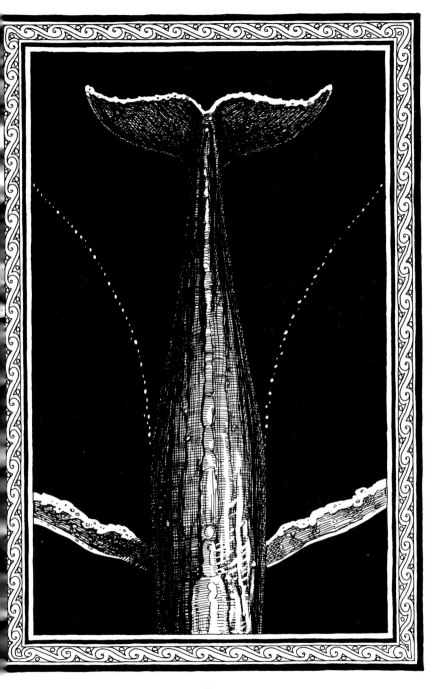

First, he killed and ate the largest fish in the ocean. Then, he hunted a giant squid. A mighty battle raged as the two monsters grappled and thrashed in the water. The giant squid tightened its tentacles around the whale, while Baleen twisted and turned until he was able to use his long, pointed teeth on the squid.

Before long, Baleen could find nothing in the sea to match his power and strength. He was the ruler of the ocean, yet he still liked to prove it. Huge and ferocious, he constantly prowled, relentless in his search for quarry.

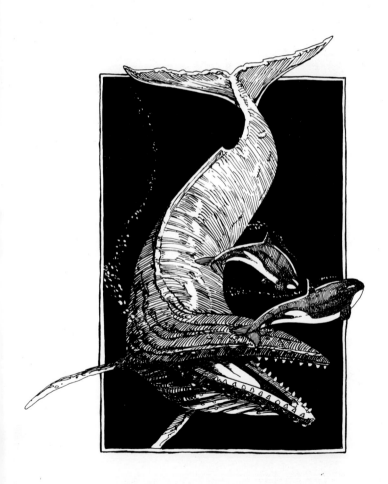

One day, as he entered deeper waters, Baleen noticed another large whale. Stealthily, he swam toward it, just as it surfaced with its mouth full of cuttlefish.

Baleen paused to stare, balancing himself with his long, paddle-like flippers.

13

The other whale was huge.

His head was like a mountain and his body long and firm. What a challenge it would be to fight *him*. What glory for the winner!

Slowly, Baleen approached.

It was forbidden for whales to fight each other. He knew that. The giant whale was a brother of sorts. But, Baleen's eye was as cold as ice. Once more, he would prove his might.

Cunningly, he moved away.

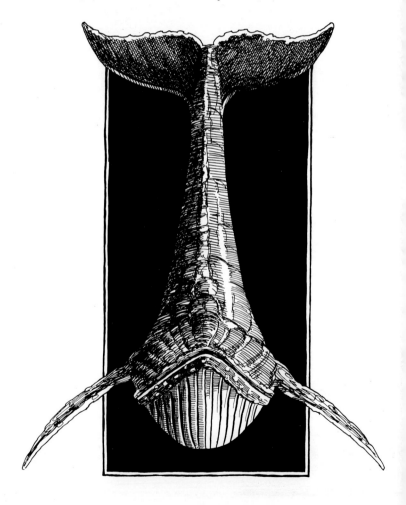

17

Then, going out some distance, he swam in a circle to return at full speed. He whacked his tail on the water, churning it with menace. He took a mighty breath, then spouted high into the air.

19

Bluntt, the massive whale, turned too late. Baleen was upon him. Baleen closed his wide jaws on a flipper and his sharp teeth tore a section free.

23

Bluntt rolled in the waves. Hurt and bleeding, he drew away, then swung himself around. The first attack had surprised him; the next one would find him prepared.

But, a new surprise awaited him.

As he hung there, poised and waiting at the water's surface, his tiny eye widened with astonishment. Instead of attacking, Baleen was twisting and turning, thrashing from side to side in the sea. His mighty mouth opened suddenly and out spilled all his teeth, splintered and broken to pieces. A strange sound came from his throat, as though he were choking.

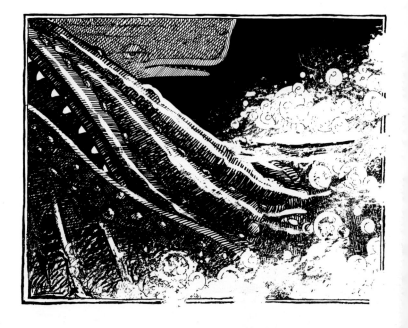

Baleen *was* choking.

A bone he had snatched out of Bluntt's flipper was wedged across his throat and would not come free. He thrashed violently, desperate to move it, desperate to breathe.

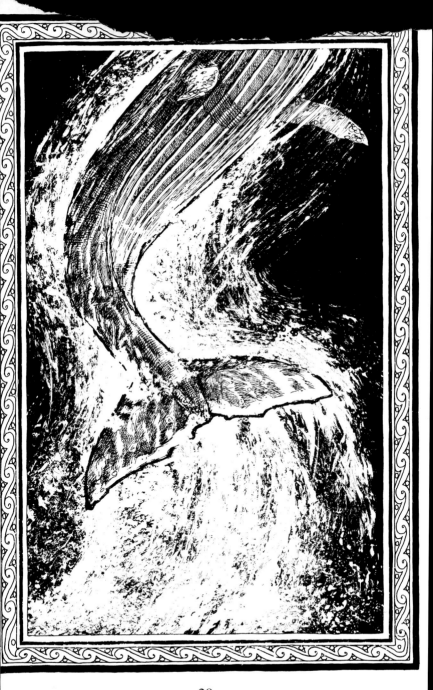

Bluntt swam toward him. His attacker was helpless now. What happened next was up to him, Bluntt.

Swiftly, he swam to Baleen's side.

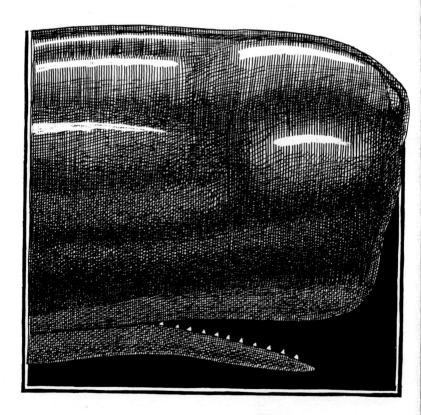

He took a deep breath, then dived beneath Baleen. Using all his great strength, Bluntt pushed and heaved until, at last, he raised Baleen's head out of the water.

33

A rush of air rasped past the piece of bone. The tremors in Baleen's body subsided as the air he needed moved once more into his lungs. Then, as Baleen's body relaxed, Bluntt moved to one side and swam away.

Baleen heard him go.

He rested, breathing painfully, silently weeping with shame. All alone, Baleen began to sing. No more would he sing a song of pride, boasting of victories won. A new song formed in Baleen's throat, echoing the pain of his shame. Beautiful and sad, the notes spilled into the water, telling the tale of the whale who had helped him. Then, from somewhere far off, sounds reached him, as though others were singing, too.

From that time on, Baleen became known for his gentleness, as are the giant whales of today. Still, the haunting notes of his song resound through the ocean depths as whales call to and answer each other.

And, to this very day, there are two kinds of whales. There are those like Bluntt, who have teeth, and those like Baleen, who have none. Like Baleen, these whales have a bone wedged across their throats, so they are forced to feed humbly upon the very, *very*, smallest creatures of the sea.

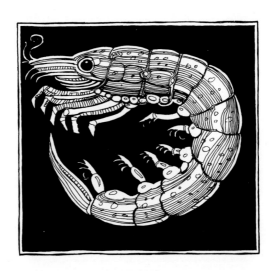

APPENDIX

Some Facts About Whales

All whales are mammals, and so have warm blood. They mate and produce live young, which drink milk from their mothers.

Instead of arms, whales have flippers. All whales have a tail with two horizontal sections called *flukes*. Some whales have a back fin called a *dorsal fin*.

There are two main groups of whales – *baleen whales* and *toothed whales*. Today, there are 11 known species of baleen whales and about 30 species of toothed whales. Baleen and toothed whales differ in several ways.

Baleen whales	Toothed whales
• have plates of baleen (whalebone) that hang down from the upper jaw and sieve food from the water	• have teeth that are usually all the same size and shape. They keep the same set of teeth throughout their life.
• may use sonar, but if so, to a lesser degree than the toothed whales	• use sonar to explore their surroundings. The sounds they use are called *clicks*.
• move from food-rich waters to breeding waters, which may mean going without food for many months	• tend to stay in food-rich waters throughout the year
• have no recorded live mass strandings	• some species are sometimes seen in live mass strandings
• are usually born headfirst (not definitely known)	• mostly seem to be born tailfirst
• mainly eat krill	• mainly eat squid, octopus, cuttlefish, and fish
• make sounds, including moans, rumbles, and chirps	• make sounds, including whistles, clicks, and groans

Baleen Whales

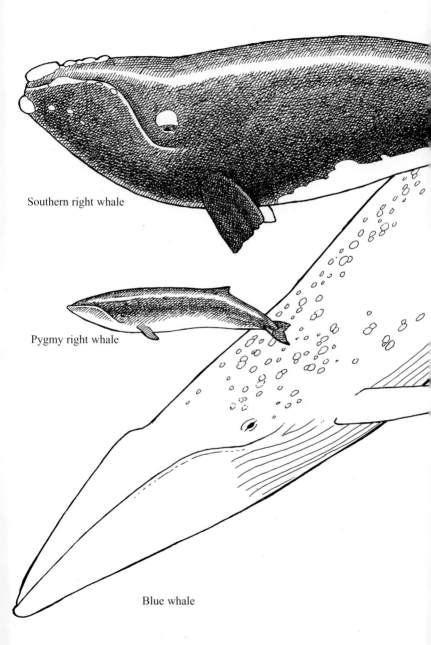

Southern right whale

Pygmy right whale

Blue whale

Southern right whale (44–56 feet) Feeds on krill. Found in cold, but usually not polar, waters in summer (feeding season); found in warmer waters, often near coasts, in winter (breeding season).

Called *right* because it was the "right" one for whalers to kill. It swims slowly, yields much oil and whalebone, plus floats when dead, making it easy to tow. Hunting greatly reduced its numbers, almost to extinction. Has been protected since 1935, but its numbers are still low.

Pygmy right whale (about 23 feet) Feeds on krill. Baleen plates filter out very small creatures. Feeds at the surface with mouth partly open, but also in mid-water and at the sea floor. Found in cold, but not polar, waters of the Southern Hemisphere.

Has not been exploited by people. Occasionally, they become tangled in fishing nets. Not a great deal is known about the pygmy right whale.

Blue whale (82–85 feet, female up to 108 feet) Feeds on krill. Found in all oceans, but usually not near coastlines. Often travels thousands of miles each year. Feeds in cold waters during summer and migrates to warm waters during winter to breed.

Largest of all whales and the largest animal known to have lived on Earth. Can weigh as much as 15 small cars.

Baleen Whales (continued)

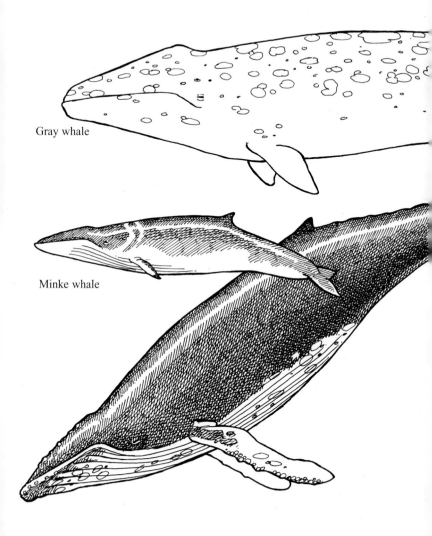

Gray whale

Minke whale

Humpback whale

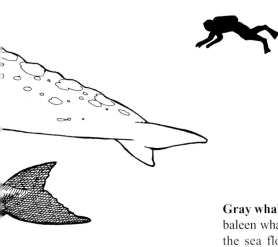

Humpback whale (52 feet) Feeds on krill and fish in shoals. Gulps water where food is concentrated, then squeezes it out, using its baleen to keep back food. Sometimes creates a curtain of bubbles that fish cannot swim through, then gulps. Often found near land as it migrates along coasts.

Name comes from the whale's habit of surfacing, then bending its back before diving. Has the largest flippers of any whale — flipper length is one third its body length. The male produces and repeats complicated "songs."

Gray whale (42–46 feet) The only baleen whale that feeds mainly on the sea floor. Found only in the northern Pacific Ocean. Lives in shallow waters near coasts and sieves tiny animals out of the sand or mud.

Skin is mottled and often has yellowish patches of barnacles. Hunting has greatly reduced its numbers.

Minke whale (26–33 feet) Feeds on krill. Found in all oceans, from polar waters to the tropics.

Named after a whaler by the name of Meineke. The minke whale is the smallest of the *rorqual whales* — whales that have grooves beneath the lower jaw, allowing skin to stretch during feeding. The minke can take in tons of sea water, then force it out through its baleen to catch krill.

Toothed Whales

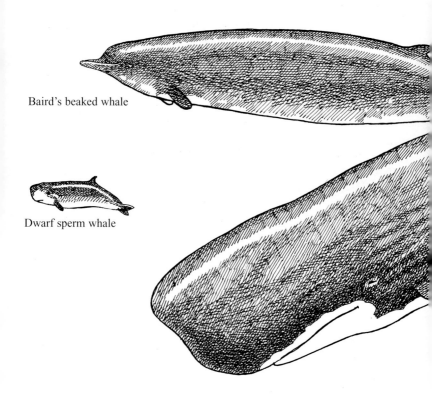

Baird's beaked whale

Dwarf sperm whale

Baird's beaked whale, also called **bottlenose whale** (up to 41 feet) Feeds mainly from ocean floor. Eats squid, octopuses, crustaceans, and fish. Found in the northern Pacific Ocean.

Largest of the beaked whales. Has four teeth, all in the lower jaw. It is thought that some males live for 80 years or more, which is longer than most other whales.

Dwarf sperm whale (less than 10 feet) Feeds on cuttlefish, squid, and fish. Found in warm and tropical seas along the edge of the continental shelf.

Smallest of all whales. Can protect itself by producing a screen of feces in the water. However, many get caught in fishing nets. Not much is known about this whale.

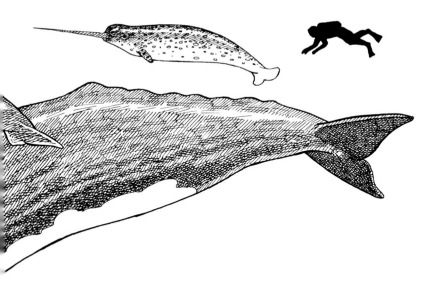

Sperm whale

Sperm whale (male up to 66 feet, female 40 feet) Feeds mainly on squid. Found in deep oceans, from polar to tropical regions.

Largest of the toothed whales. The head of an adult sperm male may be one third of its total body length. Only the lower jaw has teeth. Dives deeper than any other mammal (up to 1.2 miles). Can stay underwater for up to 90 minutes.

Narwhal (10 feet, excluding tusk) Feeds on cuttlefish, small fish, and crustaceans. Found in arctic waters.

The adult narwhal has two teeth, both in the upper jaw. In the male, the left tooth forms a spiral tusk 6–10 feet long. The purpose of the tusk is not well understood — it may be used for finding food on the sea floor or as a weapon. The narwhal is still hunted by some people for food and for its tusk. It does not survive well in captivity.

45

Toothed Whales (continued)

False killer whale

Short-finned pilot whale

False killer whale (up to 20 feet) Feeds on large fish, but also attacks smaller whales, dolphins, and porpoises. Found in all tropical and warm waters.

Lives in large groups, which often strand themselves on beaches. Adapts well to captivity. It is believed that the false killer whale takes bait from fishing nets.

Short-finned pilot whale (about 20 feet) Feeds mainly on squid. Found in warm to tropical seas.

Often mistaken for the false killer whale due to its similar size, but has a more rounded head and sloping dorsal fin. Lives in groups. Sometimes individuals swim beside each other, forming lines a few miles long in the ocean. Groups often strand themselves on beaches in large numbers.

Southern bottlenose whale

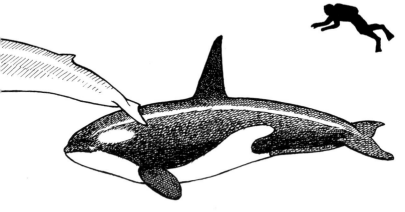

Killer whale

Southern bottlenose whale
(about 26 feet) Feeds mainly
on squid. Found in cool to
cold waters in the Southern
Hemisphere.

The *melon*, or front part of its
head, is rounded and may even
overhang the beak. Is possibly a
deep diver. Very little is known
of its biology.

Killer whale, also called **orca**
(up to 30 feet) Feeds on other
mammals (seals, sea lions, and
more), squid, fish, sharks, and
turtles. Found in all oceans,
from polar to tropical waters.

Has a distinctive dorsal fin
— nearly six feet high on adult
males, but much shorter on
females. Lives in a group called
a *pod*. Sometimes hunts in a
pack of 20 to 30 whales, using
methods like wolves or lions.
May even attack other whales,
including the huge blue whale.
Has not been known to attack
humans.

Glossary

baleen, also called **whalebone** Plates of fingernail-like material called *keratin*, which hang down from the roof of the mouth in certain whales. May be up to 400 plates on each side, each plate with a hairy fringe to help filter out tiny organisms for food.

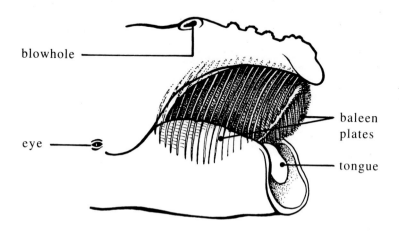

blowhole

eye

baleen plates

tongue

blowhole nostril of whale; often located far back on top of head
crustaceans mainly aquatic animals with a hard shell or crust that is shed and reformed as they grow; includes crabs, crayfish, lobsters, prawns, and shrimp
cuttlefish marine mollusks related to squid, but usually smaller
krill tiny floating animals (mainly crustaceans) that live in great numbers in some parts of the sea